It's a beautiful day at Linco[ln]
Jason and his friends are having fun
kicking a ball to one another.

What's your name?

_____

Jason is happy playing ball.

Draw a face showing how you feel today.

Art by Peter Winter

Copyright © 1995 James Boulden   Printed in USA
Boulden Publishing; P.O.Box 1186, Weaverville, CA 96093; Phone (800) 238-8433

The ball goes flying when Jason gives it an extra big kick. Jason is surprised how far he kicked the ball.

What is your favorite game at school?
(Questions are for oral discussion. No write-in blanks provided.)

The ball rolls over to where Mark is playing.

Mark starts playing with the ball and won't give it back to Jason.

How do you think Jason feels?

Jason starts calling Mark names like "dumb" and "stupid."
Mark calls Jason even worse names.

The boys start yelling louder and louder.

Will calling names get the ball back? Why?

Other kids gather around.
They think Jason and Mark may fight.

Jason doesn't want to fight, but he is afraid the kids will laugh at him if he walks away.

How do you think Mark is feeling?

Mark and Jason start pushing and shoving each other.

An adult comes over to break up the fight.

Who do you think will get to play with the ball now? Why?

Mark and Jason are sent to the principal for fighting.

The principal calls their parents.

How do you think the boys feel now?

Jason's mom is waiting for him when he gets home.
She tells Jason to clean his room after he does his homework. No TV.

What would your mom or dad say to you?

Jason gets bored and there is no TV.

He starts to think about
how things have gone from bad to worse.
He wonders what he could have done different.

*How could Jason have kept all these
bad things from happening?*

That night Jason remembers the good times he and Mark have had together.

He decides that having the ball is no big deal and not worth all this trouble.

What would you do now if you were Jason?

Jason wishes he had refused to fight.

He could have looked Mark right in the eye and then slowly walked away, keeping his back straight and head held high.

How would you feel about walking away from a fight?

Another thing Jason could have done was call an adult.

The adult would have helped Mark and Jason work things out before they got into trouble.

How would you feel about calling an adult when another kid does something wrong to you?

The adult might have suggested Mark and Jason share the ball.
Then they would both get to play with it.

Mark decides that next time he will offer to share and then there won't be a fight.

Why is sharing a good way to stop arguments?

Jason sees Mark at school the next day and tells him the ball was no big deal. It's fun to share.

Mark says he would like to be friends again.

What are you going to do the next time you get into an argument over who gets to play with something?

ROLE PLAYING — CONFLICT RESOLUTION

Conflict 1: Jennifer is jumping rope with her friend, Nadia. Sue comes over and says they should go climb on the jungle gym. Jennifer calls Sue a pest and tells her to go away. Sue calls Jennifer a spoiled brat.

- Sue: *You are a spoiled brat. You think you are special just because you have new clothes all the time. You try to keep the other kids from playing with me.*
- Jennifer: *You are a real pest, Sue. No one asked you to play with us. Just leave us alone!*

Conflict 2: Amy cuts in front of Bobby in the lunch line so she can be with her friends. Bobby shoves her out of the way. Amy pushes back and a fight starts.

- Bobby: *Go to the end of the line, stupid.*
- Amy: *You are stupid. I was in line and left to get a drink. This is my place.*

CONTRIBUTING EDITORS TO THIS PUBLICATION

Paula Aguiar
Mary Alice Birchard
Rosemary Burton
Margaret Charlton
Carla Clay
Audrey Girard
Donna Hallworth
Melinda Irwin
Cyndy Lum
Rebecca Miller
Alison Morrow
Beverly Nelson,
Donna Newell
Kathy Newbraugh
Constance Porter
Charlotte Rundell
Elisabeth Tatum
Nonnie Weeks
Dianne Williams

Special thanks to Lynne Namka of Talk, Trust and Feel, Therapeutics

ADDITIONAL RESOURCES FOR CHILDREN IN DISTRESS

Activity books, coloring books, reproducible workbooks, draw-a-face packs, game packs, videos, feelings posters & sweatshirts.

DIVORCE, BEREAVEMENT, SELF-ESTEEM, REMARRIAGE, BLENDED FAMILY, SINGLE PARENT, BULLY & VICTIM, FEELINGS, PARENTAL SUBSTANCE ABUSE, PHYSICAL & VERBAL ABUSE, SEXUAL ABUSE, AIDS, FAMILY ILLNESS, ANGER MANAGEMENT, CONFLICT RESOLUTION, COMMUNICATION.

Phone (800)238-8433 for free brochure.

Boulden Publishing; P.O. Box 1186, Weaverville, CA 96093